Distinctions in Nature

Perennial Plants and Annual Plants Explained

Shirley Duke

Cavendish Square

New York

Published in 2017 by Cavendish Square Publishing, LLC
243 5th Avenue, Suite 136, New York, NY 10016

Copyright © 2017 by Cavendish Square Publishing, LLC

First Edition

Library of Congress Cataloging-in-Publication Data

Names: Duke, Shirley Smith.
Title: Perennial plants and annual plants explained / Shirley Duke.
Description: New York : Cavendish Square Publishing, [2017] |
Series: Distinctions in nature | Includes index.
Identifiers: LCCN 2016003419 (print) | LCCN 2016012256 (ebook) |
ISBN 9781502617743 (pbk.) | ISBN 9781502617422 (library bound) |
ISBN 9781502617576 (6 pack) | ISBN 9781502617491 (ebook)
Subjects: LCSH: Perennials–Juvenile literature. | Annuals (Plants)–Juvenile literature. |
Plants–Juvenile literature.
Classification: LCC SB434 .D85 2017 (print) | LCC SB434 (ebook) |
DDC 635.9/32–dc23
LC record available at http://lccn.loc.gov/2016003419

Editorial Director: David McNamara
Editor: Kelly Spence
Copy Editor: Nathan Heidelberger
Art Director: Jeffrey Talbot
Designer: Stephanie Flecha
Production Assistant: Karol Szymczuk
Photo Research: J8 Media

Printed in the United States of America

Contents

Mint is a popular plant that is used to flavor teas, salads, and desserts.

Introduction: The World of Flowers

A garden of flowers is a beautiful sight. But plants are not just for enjoying. They have a job to do. Plants help make the **oxygen** all living things need to survive. They are also a food source for many people and some animals. Squash blossoms, garlic blossoms, and lavender are all flowers people can eat.

Classifying Flowers

Botany is the science of plants. People who study plants are called **botanists**. They

There are several different kinds of roses. Although they differ in how they look, all roses have the same structures for forming seeds.

classify, or arrange, plants into groups. These groups are based on how the plants are alike.

Flowering plants make up the largest group. They are called **angiosperms** and grow from seeds. Scientists

Zoom In

Seeds spread in different ways. Some seeds are sticky. They cling to an animal's fur or feet. Other seeds are light and can float on the wind. When the wind stops, the seeds drop. Other seeds taste good. Animals eat these seeds, and then pass the seeds as waste. Seeds may fall into water and float a long way. Some seeds travel in seed pods that pop open. The seeds scatter far from the parent plant.

further classify plants in this group by their **life cycles**. A life cycle is the different stages a living thing passes through during its lifetime.

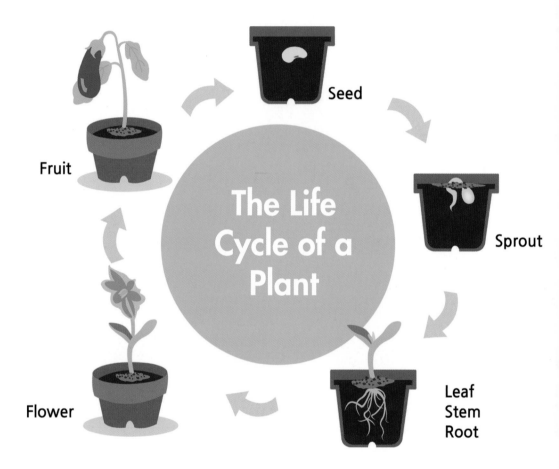

The Life Cycle of a Plant

Seed

Sprout

Leaf
Stem
Root

Flower

Fruit

Many foods, like eggplants, grow from the flower of a plant.

1 From Seed to Flower

All flowering plants follow the same basic steps in their life cycle. They start as seeds. To grow, a seed needs water, oxygen, and warm weather. Now the seed can **germinate**, or sprout. The roots grow down and the stem grows up. The new plant is called a seedling. After the seedling is fully grown, it produces flowers. The flowers make seeds through **fertilization**. Sometimes the seeds form inside a fruit. New plants grow from these seeds.

Three Groups

Flowering plants are classified into three groups. Each group follows a different pattern during its life cycle. These life cycles also last for different lengths of time. Some plants have a short lifespan, while others live for many years.

Zoom In

Each flower has a male part called a stamen. The stamen makes pollen. Pollination takes place when pollen from the stamen is carried to another flower. There, it mixes with the pistil, or the female part of a flower. This process allows fertilization to take place. Fertilization is how seeds form.

Annuals complete their life cycle in one season. **Biennials** have a two-year life cycle. Plants that live for three or more years are classified as **perennials**.

The showy peony stamens almost hide the flower's pistil and look similar to its petals.

Begonias are an easy-to-grow annual that fill gardens with color. These plants need good soil and plenty of water to thrive.

2 Looking at Life Cycles

Let's take a closer look at plant life cycles.

Annuals

Annuals start as seeds that produce leaves, blossom, and then grow seeds. All these steps take place in one season. By the end of the growing season, only the new seeds are left. Fresh plants will grow from these seeds the following year. Geraniums, marigolds, and petunias are examples of annuals.

Annuals grow quickly so they can produce seeds. They make many seeds so more flowers

As bees gather pollen, some of the yellow dust is carried from one flower to another, pollinating the plants.

The biennial cotton thistle forms a rosette in its first year. The next year it develops into a tall, spiny plant.

will grow the next year. Annuals usually have bright, showy flowers. These colorful blooms attract insects. The insects help spread the plant's pollen, the dusty-looking material that helps fertilization. The plant dies in winter.

Biennials

The prefix "bi-" means "two." Biennial plants take two years to complete their life cycle. In the first year, the

Zoom In

Plants use water, air, and light from the sun to make energy. This process is called photosynthesis. The sunlight is absorbed by chlorophyll, which is the green coloring in a plant's leaves and stem. Plants use this energy to grow. Biennials store extra energy in their roots to survive the winter.

plant grows its **foliage**, or leaves. This cluster of leaves is called a **rosette**. Roots and stems also develop during the first year. During the second year, the flowers and seeds grow. Biennials are able to use most of their energy in the second year to grow flowers that

Most hollyhocks grow from seeds their first year and bloom the second year.

produce seeds. Biennials include foxgloves, hollyhocks, and sweet William.

Perennials

Perennial plants live for three or more years. Many continue to bloom year after year. Others grow for a

Asters come in many colors, including purple, pink, red, and white.

Perennial Plants and Annual Plants Explained

Bulbs are planted underground. They have five basic parts. The bottom of the bulb has a plate that the roots sprout from. Bulbs also contain fleshy scales, a papery skin, the shoot, and extra buds.

few years, blossom once, then die. Perennial flowers do not blossom as long as annuals. Perennials include asters, coneflowers, and roses.

Perennial flowers grow from seeds or **bulbs**. Bulbs are resting stems with buds surrounded by leaves. Lilies, onions, and tulips are perennials that grow from bulbs. Perennials like pinks and black-eyed Susans begin as seeds.

Bulbs, like this tulip bulb, store nutrients and energy to form leaf scales and flower buds inside so that the flower will bloom the next year.

Growing a Garden

In a garden, annuals must be planted every year. The seeds or seedlings are buried in the ground. They need water and **fertilizer**, which contains nutrients, to grow. When they die, the plant is pulled up. Biennials require the same care as annuals. They are pulled

Providing the proper care and mixing annuals, biennials, and perennials in your garden results in flowers that bloom at different times during the growing season.

after they bloom during the second year of their life cycle. Perennials require less care.

Plant Zones

The US Department of Agriculture produces a map that shows which plants grow best in certain areas. The map is based on how low the **temperature** will drop. Frost and cold weather can damage or kill certain **species** of flowers. People study the map to figure out which plants will grow well in their gardens.

Freezing temperatures or frost can quickly damage new plants. Check the Department of Agriculture map online to see what kinds of plants grow best in the area where you live.

1. Hyacinths come in many colors from snowy white to pale blue.

2. Marigolds grow best in sunny garden beds.

3 Be a Plant Detective

Use these clues to classify the plants (*left*) into their proper groups.

1. A hyacinth grows from a bulb. It will come back each year. Use the reading to decide which group this flower belongs in.

2. A marigold has bright, showy blossoms all summer long. It will die in the fall and won't return next year. It must be replanted. Is this an annual, biennial, or perennial plant?

3. Tulips store energy over the winter in structures like these so they will bloom in spring.

4. Canterbury bell blossoms can be blue, purple, white, or pink.

3. Tulips grow from a special part that contains everything needed for the tulip to grow again. The part is made of five smaller parts. What is it called?

4. By winter, a Canterbury bell has grown roots, stems, and leaves. The second year brings flowers that make seeds. What group does this flower belong to?

Answer Key:

1. Hyacinths are sweet-smelling perennials. They grow from bulbs that are planted in the fall.

2. Marigolds are annuals. These flowers have a sharp smell that keeps away many kinds of insects.

3. This is a bulb from which a tulip will grow. These colorful perennials bloom in early spring for between three and seven days.

4. A Canterbury bell is a biennial. They grow best in moist soil and can stand up to 3 feet (1 meter) high.

Tulips are perennials that require hot, dry summers and cold winters to return each year. In other climates, they are treated as annuals.

4 Rule Breakers

Not all flowers can be classified as annuals, biennials, or perennials. Some break the rules.

Testy Tulips

Tulips can be annuals or perennials. It depends on what the weather is like where they are grown. Tulips come from Asia, where they are perennials. In some parts of the United States, tulips lose their foliage early in the season. The foliage supplies the energy to make the bulb. If a tulip does not have enough stored energy, it will not bloom the next year.

Changing Groups

Some plants don't follow the pattern of normal annuals or perennials. The climate and place where they grow changes the length of their life cycle. Plants grow faster in places where the growing season is warmer and lasts longer. Geraniums are annuals in the north because of the cold winters. In the warmer south, they are perennials.

The green stems of perennial geraniums become woody as they grow older and larger.

Mix and Match

Scientists in Belgium have discovered a way to change an annual into a perennial. They were able to turn off the signal that tells annuals to grow flowers. This stopped the plants from using up all their energy. The new mutant plants are then able to live longer than one season.

Besides changing seeds, scientists also study how seeds grow in different soils and locations.

angiosperms Flowering plants.

annuals Flowers that complete their life cycle in one year.

biennials Flowers that take two years to complete their life cycle.

botanists Scientists that study and classify plants.

botany The science of plants and how they live and grow.

bulbs The resting stage of some flowers that includes a stem and buds.

chlorophyll The green coloring in plants.

classify To put or organize things with similar characteristics into groups.

fertilization The stage in a plant's life cycle where male pollen mixes with the female plant parts to form a seed.

fertilizer A substance containing nutrients that plants need to live and grow.

foliage The leaves of a plant.

germinate When a seed begins to grow with water and the right temperatures.

life cycles The different stages through which living things pass during their lifetimes.

oxygen A clear gas that is necessary for life to exist.

perennials Plants that live and return each year for three or more years.

photosynthesis The process by which plants convert light, air, and water into energy.

pistil The female part of a flower.

pollen The tiny, dust-like material on the male part of a flower.

pollination The process where pollen is put into a flower so it can form seeds.

rosette A cluster of leaves that grow during the first year of a biennial's life cycle.

seed pods The part of the plant that holds the seeds.

species Groups of living things with like characteristics that can reproduce.

stamen The male part of a flower.

temperature How hot or cold something is.

Books

Colby, Jennifer. *Flowers*. 21st Century Junior Library. North Mankato, MN: Cherry Lake Publishing, 2014.

Owens, L. L. *The Life Cycle of a Daisy*. Life Cycles. North Mankato, MN: The Child's World, 2011.

Senker, Cath. *Garden Flowers*. Adventures in Nature. New York: PowerKids Press, 2016.

Websites

DK Findout! The Life Cycle of a Plant
www.dkfindout.com/uk/video/animals-and-nature/life-cycle-plant-video
Learn about the life cycle of a nasturtium.

The Learning Garden: Annual, Perennial, or Biennial?
assoc.garden.org/courseweb/course2/week2/page4.htm
Read about the different kinds of plant life cycles.

Index

Page numbers in **boldface** are illustrations.

Shirley Duke has written more than fifty books about science and nature, but writing about life science is her specialty. A long-time gardener, she has grown annual, perennial, and biennial plants in her yard and garden. A resident of the Jemez Mountains in New Mexico, she discovered that growing plants there means keeping out the many wild animals in the neighborhood.

DATE DUE

			PRINTED IN U.S.A.